CATHARINE PARR TRAILL

CATHARINE PARR TRAILL

BACKWOODS PIONEER

Carol Martin

A GROUNDWOOD BOOK
DOUGLAS & McINTYRE
TORONTO VANCOUVER BERKELEY

Groundwood Books / Douglas & McIntyre
720 Bathurst Street, Suite 500, Toronto, Ontario M5S 2R4

We acknowledge for their financial support of our publishing program the Canada Council for the Arts, the Ontario Arts Council, the Government of Ontario through the Ontario Media Development Corporation's Ontario Book Initiative and the Government of Canada through the Book Publishing Industry Development Program (BPIDP).

ONTARIO ARTS COUNCIL
CONSEIL DES ARTS DE L'ONTARIO

National Library of Canada Cataloging in Publication
Martin, Carol
Catharine Parr Traill: backwoods pioneer / by Carol Martin.
Includes index.
ISBN 0-88899-495-8 (pbk.)
1. Traill, Catharine Parr, 1802-1899. 2. Women authors, Canadian (English)–19th century–Biography–Juvenile literature. I. Title.
PS8439.T7Z77 2004   jC813'.3   C2003-906886-2

Book design by Michael Solomon
Printed and bound in Canada

To my brother, Donald Wood,
who lives in Catharine Parr Traill country.

Contents

....

One
A Happy Childhood

CATHARINE wandered along the beach with her sisters. It was her favourite place to play, and Stowe House, the Strickland home in East Anglia, England, was only a few steps from the river. She bent down and picked up a gleaming wet stone. Every morning the tide left new treasures, and she always found something special — sometimes even a fossil or an amber pebble — to add to the family's collection.

"Come back, Katie. It's time to go home for dinner. We're already late," called Elizabeth, shouting to be heard above the wind. Thirteen-year-old Eliza was the oldest of the six sisters. She often seemed bossy, but she was responsible for them much of the time and worried that they might get into trouble.

Catharine ran to join her sisters. The oldest girls after Elizabeth — Agnes, Sarah and Jane — were each two years apart, but the youngest, Catharine and her little sister, Susanna, were only a year apart and usually played together.

The children often spent their afternoons on the shore. There was always something to see there, with the boats bobbing in the water, and the fishermen tending their nets. Catharine loved to go fishing with her father. From the time she was six, she was her father's favourite companion when he set out along the river. Soon she was trusted to take care of the fishing tackle and was happy spending hours playing by the water and gathering the flowers and strawberries that grew along the banks.

At home the children spent most of their time in the small brick-floored parlour. It was warm and dark, with oak-lined walls and a huge brick fireplace. Here they learned the lessons taught by their mother in the mornings, read and played games when it was too cold or wet outside, and were cared for by a servant who spoiled the younger children. At the end of the day, the girls put on their best white dresses, and the footman escorted them to the dining room for dessert with the adults.

Late in 1808, when Catharine was six, the Stricklands moved to Reydon Hall, in Suffolk on England's east coast, just a mile from the sea. Two little brothers had been added to the family – Samuel, now three years old, and Thomas, only one.

"Well do I remember the move to Reydon that bitter Christmas Eve," Catharine would say in later years. "The roads were deep in snow, and we children were sent over in an open tax-cart with the servants and carpenters. It was so cold they rolled me up in a velvet pelisse belonging to Eliza to keep me from freezing, but I was as merry as a cricket all the way, and kept them laughing over my childish sallies. We stopped at a place called 'Deadman's Grave' to have some straw put into the bottom of the cart to keep us warm. No, I shall never forget that journey to Reydon through the snow."

Reydon Hall was a magical place for the Strickland children to grow up in. A mansion — almost a castle — it had a gabled roof, tall chimneys, and even haunted garrets and secret chambers. It was surrounded by trees and there was a forest nearby. When the Stricklands lived there, almost two hundred years ago, the walls were covered with ivy.

The children loved playing in their new, rambling, ivy-covered home, with its winding halls, secret rooms and garrets. As Catharine remembered it, "The old Hall with its desolate garrets, darkened windows, worm-eaten floor, closed-up staircase and secret recesses might have harboured a legion of ghosts — and as for rappings, we heard plenty of them." The girls were told that mysterious relatives of the previous owners continued to haunt the building, and they terrorized the family servants by telling stories of ghosts and witchcraft.

Samuel and Thomas, as was the custom, were sent to

boarding school at an early age, but, like other girls in the early part of the nineteenth century, the six sisters were taught at home.

Mrs. Strickland taught the girls to read and write and instructed them in the other skills that were expected of young women: sewing, embroidery, sketching, proper behaviour, as well as religion and how to manage a household.

Their father, whose health was not good and who had retired from his work in London to live the life of a country gentleman, was well read and an enthusiastic teacher. It was he who gave his daughters the kind of broad education usually reserved for boys, instructing them in literature and the classics, history, arithmetic and science.

Both parents instilled in the children a love of nature, encouraging them to study the animals, insects and birds around them. The girls learned about plants and flowers and were encouraged to draw them — something in which Catharine, to her later regret, had no interest. Each had her own garden to plant and care for.

Mr. Strickland had investments to oversee in Norwich, where he owned a house. Because he suffered from gout and found it difficult to travel, it was best for him to spend the winters there, where he was often joined by his wife and one or two of his daughters. This left the younger children to be taught and cared for by Elizabeth, then about twenty years old, and the servants. They had plenty of time on their own, and they all developed a special love of books. Their father's large library was a favourite place, and reading was their main pleasure and entertainment.

Their reading wasn't much like that of young people today. There was almost no fiction in the library, and no books written for young readers. "We tried history, the drama, voyages and travels," wrote Catharine later. "We wanted to be very learned just then, but as you may imagine, we made small progress in that direction." The girls were excited when they discovered the adventures to be found in the plays of Shakespeare, and amused themselves by acting out the scenes.

In temperament Catharine and Susanna were opposites. Susanna was emotional and moody, while Catharine had a warm and affectionate nature. Susanna raged against injustice and unfair treatment in general. Catharine was more likely to accept life as it came and make the best of things. But this never interfered with their affection for each other, and they remained close friends for the rest of their lives. In an early letter to a friend, Susanna claimed, "I would rather give up the pen than lose the affection of my beloved sister Catharine, who is dearer to me than all the world."

When the two were in their early teens, Catharine wrote, "Susan and I formed the brilliant notion of writing a novel and amusing ourselves by reading aloud at night what had been written during the day. But where should we find paper? We had no pocket-money, and even if we had been amply supplied there was no place within our reach where we could purchase the means of carrying out our literary ambitions."

It is hard to imagine now, but at that time paper was a precious commodity, and writing imagined stories was frowned on, even in households such as the Stricklands'. The girls were excited when they found reams of paper and dozens of quill pens in a great chest in which all kinds of treasures had been stored. They kept their project a secret from all but Sarah, the sister closest to them in age. They knew that their mother, and especially their sister Elizabeth, would disapprove.

Each day they would write some of their story. It was set in the days of William Tell, the legendary Swiss hero who was forced by a cruel invader to shoot an apple from the head of his son. He later killed the enemy and set his people free. His bravery made him a particular hero of Catharine's. Each night the new part of the story would be read to Sarah, who provided an enthusiastic audience and gave advice.

One day, just as Catharine was reading the last of her story aloud, she later wrote, "a small white hand was quietly placed on mine and the papers extracted. I looked at Sara [as Catharine wrote her sister's name] in dismay. Not a word had been spoken, but I knew my mother's hand, and the dread of Eliza's criticism became an instant reality." The story was taken away and only returned when the girls promised to use the paper for curling papers.

Two
Making a Living

IN 1818, the year Catharine turned sixteen, the Stricklands' life changed. The depression following the Napoleonic Wars forced many companies out of business. For the Stricklands it meant the loss of their fortune and soon afterward the death of their father, both shattering blows to the family.

Catharine, Elizabeth and Agnes had been living with Mr. Strickland in Norwich at this time, to help him and to be close to their young brothers who were at boarding school nearby. After their father died, Agnes was sent to stay with friends, but the other two sisters stayed on. Both were heartbroken over their father's death. Catharine had always been his special companion when they were in the country, and Elizabeth, now twenty-four, had worked closely with her father on his business affairs.

While Elizabeth continued to manage the business details, Catharine spent many hours alone, sewing and reading. She had secretly kept one of the stories she had written a year earlier, "The Swiss Herd-boy and His Alpine Marmot." Now she began writing more short stories, including "The Blind Highland Piper" and "The Little Water-Carrier." One day, when she came back from picking red currants in the garden, her papers had disappeared from the desk. She was afraid to ask about them. Elizabeth still disapproved, and Catharine thought that perhaps she had discovered the stories and burned them.

Some days later, the sisters were visited by their guardian, who was acting in the place of their father. Mr. Morgan drew the missing pages from his pocket and said, "Eliza, I did not know you had time for story-writing." Guiltily Catharine admitted that the stories were hers. Mr. Morgan smiled and said he thought they were very good, and he wanted to take them away to correct them. What he really had in mind was to show them to a London publisher. The publisher liked them enough to have them printed and sent Catharine five golden guineas, a wonderful addition to the family finances. The stories were published as *The Tell Tale: An Original Collection of Moral and Amusing Stories*. So, at sixteen, Catharine became a published author — the first of the sisters to earn money from her writing. She was thrilled, and the whole family benefitted from the additional income.

The book was a surprising success and launched Catharine and her sisters (with the exception of Sarah, the only sister to remain uninterested in life as a writer) on literary careers. This was in 1818, when it was almost impossible for young women of the Stricklands' class in England to make a living in a profession. Women in the lower classes could work as servants or in factories, but for middle-class women such a future was unthinkable.

Catharine and Susanna. Both young women styled their hair in the curls or clusters of ringlets popular at the time. Later, as pioneers in Upper Canada, they had little time to spend on stylish hairdos. We have no pictures of either sister during their early decades as young wives and mothers in Canada, but their hair was probably drawn back out of the way in a neat bun. In later years it was covered with a bonnet – a simple one to wear around the house and a more elaborate one for special occasions.

Writing was a way for the sisters to earn a little of the money that the family needed so badly.

In spite of the long-held belief that fiction would "inflame the passions," a new attitude was beginning to develop in England. An exciting new interest in the writings of women began to take hold and, although most stories for children were still full of obvious moral lessons, fiction as we know it was beginning to develop. Soon such stories as *Oliver Twist*, *Wuthering Heights* and *Alice in Wonderland* would become popular, if daring, reading.

Agnes had already been successful in having a poem printed, and the Strickland sisters, including Elizabeth, began to see writing as a way out of their poverty. Over the next few years, four of the five sisters began to devote their energies to writing. They concentrated, for the most part, on historical or other non-fiction material.

Catharine was soon producing manuscripts for a number of publishers. They were mostly moral stories intended to teach young people lessons about behaviour, or short pieces about nature such as "Little Downy, the Field-mouse," or "The History of a Field-mouse: A Moral Tale," one of her most popular stories.

Many of Catharine's stories were published in annual collections, the popular books of stories that came out each year just before Christmas. Over the next twelve years, at least twelve of her books were published, as well as many articles and stories. It is difficult to be more

"Little Downy, the Field-mouse" was based on a real mouse Catharine liked to watch as he ran about under the oak tree outside their house. She made notes on a slate she carried with her, then copied them into her notebook later. Although the story includes many details of the imagined life of a field mouse, it is full of lessons:

Remember, my little Alfred, that idleness is the root of all evil, as you may see in the case of Downy: — now which do you think was the happiest and best, — careful and industrious Downy making her house, and busily procuring food for herself against the winter, — or careless idle Downy doing nothing but playing and enjoying herself in the garden, eating the fruit and sleeping among the flowers?

exact since, for a time, both Catharine and Susanna followed the custom of not having their names on the books and stories they wrote. They were usually described as being "by a Lady," or "by the author of [the previous story]." Susanna had various titles published under the initials "S.S." or "Z.Z."

Without Mr. Strickland and the income they had once had, life was very difficult for the whole family. By now, Elizabeth and Catharine had moved back to Reydon Hall where the family lived quietly and in near poverty for some years. They occupied only a small part of the big house, closing most of it to keep costs down. A local writer once described a visit he made to the family:

> The Stricklands had, I fancy, seen better days… and I well remember the feeling of surprise with which I first entered their capacious drawing-room… It must have been, now I come to think of it, a dismal old house, suggestive of rats and dampness and mould, that Reydon Hall, with its scantily furnished rooms and its unused attics and its empty barns and stables, with a general air of decay all over the place.

Samuel and Thomas were growing up. Perhaps they found the quiet restricted life in a household full of women boring. Perhaps they felt that it was their duty to make their own way in the world. At any rate, soon both left home. The family had lost their servants, including the gardeners, with the loss of their fortune, but they worked in the vegetable garden themselves and were able to provide much of their own food. With only this experience, Sam, at the age of twenty, set out for the colonies in 1825 to try his hand at farming in the wilds of Upper Canada. A few months later, Thomas, then only eighteen, joined the famous East India Company. Within a few years, he was made captain of his own ship.

Meanwhile, the women continued to do their best to bring much-needed money into the household with their writing.

THREE
Excitement and Romance in London

I N NINETEENTH-CENTURY England, people kept strictly to their own class, and the Stricklands, living close to poverty, were no longer welcome in the class of country society that they were accustomed to. Instead, they began to make new friends among those of the intellectual class who shared their interest in books and writing. Before long the writing of the sisters became known in London, the literary centre of the country.

Within a few years, first Elizabeth and then Catharine and Susanna moved to London. Not, of course, to live by themselves. It would have been scandalous at the time for young, single women to live on their own, or even with each other. Instead they stayed as guests with relatives or friends.

Susanna was a passionate supporter of political causes, and this was a time when thoughtful people were beginning to recognize how abhorrent slavery was and to fight for its abolition. She took up the struggle, joined the Anti-Slavery League and wrote pamphlets on its behalf. Through friendships with other league members, she met and fell in love with John Dunbar Moodie. He was one of England's half-pay retired army officers who had acquired free land in South Africa. He had returned to England in the hope of finding a wife to take back with him, and perhaps raising some money from his English relatives. He was writing a book about his experiences and swept Susanna off her feet with his tales of the exciting life to be found in South Africa. A passionate woman like Susanna, a writer full of stimulating ideas and hopes for the future, appealed greatly to him. In the fall of 1830 the two were married.

By now Agnes, Jane, Catharine and Susanna were all writing books, poetry, stories and pamphlets, with Elizabeth acting as their editor. In spite of the restrictions women in the early decades of the nineteenth century lived under, the social and cultural world was beginning to open up to them. Mary Wollstonecraft had written her controversial essay, "Vindication of the Rights of Woman," a few decades earlier, and Jane Austen's novels (four of them published anonymously) were already famous.

Although the sisters' literary careers were progressing nicely, they were not as successful in finding husbands and creating their own homes. Susanna was torn between her love for John Moodie and the happiness she had found in London. She actually called off the engagement for a time. Then Catharine, who had become engaged to Francis Harral, the son of one of her literary friends, suffered her first serious heartbreak. Neither Catharine nor Francis had money of their own or any prospects for making their way financially in the world. Francis's mother opposed the marriage, urging him to seek a wife with money of her own. The engagement ended, leaving both deeply unhappy.

Catharine, typically, spoke little of her unhappiness. A London cousin, Rebecca Leverton, took her on a trip to Bath and Oxford to help her forget, and she stayed very busy. Most of her time was spent with friends or relatives, making herself useful by helping out in any way she could. At Mrs. Leverton's she would rise at dawn, skim the milk in the dairy for the cream, take a warm glass to her cousin in bed, perhaps sew or organize the shopping, then join Mrs. Leverton on her social visits and end the evening with a game or two of draughts or backgammon after a final visit to the dairy. She also kept up her writing. Most of her books at this time were about nature, written for young readers, such as *Sketches from Nature; or Hints to Juvenile Naturalists*. As with most books for young readers of the time, they were informative but had a strong moral tone.

In spite of the pleasures found in the literary world, writers received little or nothing for their work, and life in England at that time did not offer much for young people without careers or family money. For many, the idea of picking up and moving to the colonies — South Africa, Australia or Canada — seemed to offer a more exciting future. As Susanna later wrote, a "Canadian mania" swept through England during those years. The country was widely promoted, there were lectures on its beauty and the opportunities there, and free land was offered to the young men who had returned from the Napoleonic Wars.

Many of these ex-military men, particularly the younger sons of upper-class families, began to dream of making a life for themselves in one of the new countries. (Such sons could not expect to inherit land and so were

Napoleonic Wars

The end of the eighteenth century was a time of revolution throughout Europe and North America. The class structure that had for centuries kept the poorest people from improving their lives was undermined by the new idea that all people should have equal rights.

Napoleon came to power in France in 1799. Although his attempt to conquer the rest of Europe ended with defeat in 1815, the wars led to social and political changes that were permanent. For the British it meant a disruption of trade with Europe, which destroyed many businesses, including those of Catharine's father.

When the war ended, the young British men who had served in Europe found themselves without work. Many were retired with partial pay as "half-pay officers." A number saw no future for themselves in Britain and emigrated to other parts of the empire, such as South Africa, Australia or North America, where settlers were in demand and received free land and sometimes even free transportation.

For North America, the war had a number of results. To raise the money he needed, Napoleon sold a huge area drained by the Mississippi River, known as the Louisiana Territory, to the United States. In Canada, the British need for large timbers for the masts of their warships led to the development of the Canadian forest industry. On the high seas, British ships were attacking American ships and seizing their cargoes to stop goods from reaching France. In 1812, in retaliation, the Americans declared war on Britain, including the Canadian colony. When the war ended in 1815, the British and Canadians had been successful in protecting the country from invasion, marking the beginning of Canadian nationalism.

at a serious disadvantage socially and financially.) In England all the land was already owned, and most interesting work was controlled by those in positions of power. In the colonies everything was new, and it seemed that anything was possible if one was willing to work hard. John Moodie, who had always planned to return to South Africa, began to consider Canada instead. He and Susanna spent many evenings talking about making the trip. After all, Samuel Strickland was already there and happily settled with his own family. He could help them get started.

The decision was a particularly difficult one for Susanna. She loved being with her friends in London and taking part in the literary life and her causes there. She knew that life in the colonies would be quite different. She and John nearly broke up over this, but in the end she decide that life as Mrs. Moodie was what she wanted — even if it meant leaving behind everything she knew.

Only one thing made them delay their departure. Susanna was pregnant. They would have to wait until after the baby was born.

In the meantime Catharine met Thomas Traill. He and Susanna's husband had been childhood friends on the Orkney Islands north of Scotland. They had served together in the final years of the Napoleonic Wars and left the army as half-pay officers. Thomas was thirty-nine, a widower and the father of two teenage sons who were being raised by their mother's family back home in the Orkneys. He and Catharine were immediately attracted and were soon making their own plans to marry.

THE

YOUNG EMIGRANTS;

OR,

PICTURES OF CANADA.

CALCULATED TO

AMUSE AND INSTRUCT THE MINDS OF

YOUTH.

BY THE AUTHOR OF

" *Prejudice Reproved*," " *The Tell-tale*," &c.

London :

PRINTED FOR HARVEY AND DARTON,
GRACECHURCH-STREET.

1826.

The Young Emigrants

Most of Catharine's book about the experiences of a family settling in Upper Canada is written in the form of letters to a sister in England. The style is very different from what we are used to today, but the story is full of accurate information about the country and its plant and animal life. In this short excerpt, Agnes writes to her sister Ellen about her changing attitude towards fashion:

I remember, I used once to place the utmost importance on the smartness of my dress, the fashion of my bonnet, and the shape of my gown; but now my dress is cut to the most convenient shape; and my chief study in choosing a hat, is to suit it to the different seasons of the year. And, indeed, I am quite as well pleased with my dark stuff and blue cotton gowns, and with my checked or linseywoolsey apron, as I was formerly in wearing the finest muslin or richest silk. I think I see my sister smile at my change of ideas, and hear her exclaim, "A blue cotton gown and checked apron!" Yes, dearest Ellen, this is my winter's attire, and I am quite reconciled to wearing it. Indeed, were I to do otherwise, I should be laughed at for affecting a singularity of dress.

Although Thomas's age (he was nine years older than Catharine), lack of prospects and his two children meant that Catharine's family were not in favour of it, the two were married in May of 1832. "He is all that a faithful heart can want in a partner for life," she wrote to a friend on her wedding day.

Catharine and Thomas made their own decision to emigrate to Canada quickly. The two couples had probably discussed the possibilities of creating a better future there. Catharine entered into the plans with more enthusiasm than Susanna. She was quite knowledgeable about the country from the letters that had come from friends and from her brother Sam. She had even written a book for children on the experiences of a family that had lost most of their income and had moved to the new country to try their luck there. Entitled *The Young Emigrants: or, Pictures of Canada: Calculated to Amuse and Instruct the Minds of Youth*, it describes the trip across the ocean and the arrival of the family on the land they were to settle.

In May of 1832, shortly after the wedding, the Traills were packed and on their way. But first they had to travel to the Orkneys to introduce Catharine to Thomas's children and his family. Leaving her mother and her sisters was difficult for Catharine. She must have suspected that she might never again see those who remained behind — and she never did. But the family always remained close, writing back and forth frequently and working together on publishing projects.

FOUR

Crossing the Sea to the New World

D URING THE TRIP through Scotland, Catharine became ill, and, on July 7, 1832, she was carried aboard the *Laurel*, and the long voyage began. Although she was sick much of the way, she made little of it in her account of the voyage or her letters home.

In the early 1800s, crossing the Atlantic was a slow and often dangerous experience. The ship Catharine and Thomas travelled on was not primarily designed for passengers. Catharine saw this as a benefit. The passenger ships tended to be crammed with immigrants, many already carrying diseases. There was little food and sometimes even that was rotten; the air in the hold and the drinking water were both bad. No wonder they were referred to as "coffin ships"! In contrast, the *Laurel* carried only two other passengers — the teenaged nephew of the captain and a young man whom Catharine described as "too much wrapped up in his own affairs to be very communicative to others."

For weeks there was little to do, and Catharine was soon bored with the inactivity, the lack of space and what little there was to read in the ship's library. She realized,

James, a Canadian-built brig of the 1830s, probably much like the one in which Catharine and Thomas crossed the Atlantic.

however, that the trip was even more frustrating for Thomas. "I really do pity men who are not actively employed: women have always their needle as a resource against the overwhelming weariness of an idle life: but where a man is confined to a small space, such as the deck and cabin of a trading vessel, with nothing to see, nothing to hear, nothing to do, and nothing to read, he is really a very pitiable creature."

Catharine did spend some of her time sewing after she had recovered from the pangs of seasickness. And sometimes she sat on a bench on the deck and watched the sea birds swoop and glide over the waves. The bench was covered with cloaks for her comfort, and beneath it was a coop for the chickens that were part of the journey's food supply. "Poor prisoners," she thought, "to be killed and cooked as needed!"

They had been sailing for a whole month before the *Laurel* came within sight of Newfoundland. (Susanna and her husband, who had left Scotland a week earlier than the Traills, were not nearly so lucky. The trip took them two months!) It was exciting for everyone on board to sail up the broad St. Lawrence. A "majestic river," wrote Catharine, "it seems an ocean in itself." They charted their passage past islands, hills and mountains on the captain's map, noting the new birds that came to call and smelling the fresh scent of plants and flowers on the air.

One morning they stopped at a small island and, although the captain would not allow Catharine to go ashore, Thomas brought her a bouquet of flowers from the new continent. She was quick to identify and compare them with flowers from home: roses, pulmonaria, others she did not recognize, and even wild orchids. She quickly pressed them for study, as she was in the habit of doing back home in England.

Eleven days after first sighting land, they anchored at Grosse Isle, where passengers from all ships were checked for infectious diseases such as smallpox, typhoid fever and cholera. Those who were ill were taken to the quarantine hospital for which the island was famous.

Once more the captain forced Catharine to remain aboard in order to protect her from disease, but the island doctor, who met her when he inspected the ship, had strawberries, raspberries and flowers sent back for her. That night she saw the lights of Quebec City.

After six more days, the ship arrived at Montreal.

Catharine was delighted with her first view of the "glittering steeples and roofs of the city, with its gardens and villas... It looked lovely by the softened glow of a Canadian summer sunset," she wrote.

But cholera had devastated Montreal that year. New arrivals, weakened by the long voyage, were in particular danger. In fact the disease usually arrived on the overcrowded, badly outfitted ships. In house after house whole families died. Many others had fled the city.

Before the Traills could be on their way the next day, Catharine, still recovering from her earlier sickness, became one of cholera's victims. In typical form, she covers this terrifying period in a few sentences in her letter home and praises the kindness of the Irish girls who cared for her during her "violent fits of sickness." The doctor's treatment included "bleeding [a common practice of the day], a portion of opium, blue pill, and some sort of salts." There was no cure for the disease. Patients either recovered on their own or died.

Catharine's best-known book, *The Backwoods of Canada*, based on her journals and letters home, describes her experiences during the voyage and her family's first years as pioneers in Upper Canada.

The Dreaded Cholera

Cholera was one of the most feared diseases of the nineteenth century. It was horrifying. Patients died, racked by pain, with vile liquids pouring from their bodies. Half of those who were struck died within a day or two. With the increased traffic of ships from continent to continent, cholera had travelled around the world from India, where it was first diagnosed, leaving death in its wake. The Traills reached Montreal in August, 1832, during one of the worst periods of the epidemic. Two thousand of the city's population of 32,000 died that year. "In some situations," wrote Catharine, "whole streets had been nearly depopulated; those that were able fled panic-stricken to the country villages, while others remained to die in the bosom of their families."

This cartoon printed in the *Canadian Illustrated News* depicts death riding through the streets of Montreal when cholera, fever and smallpox were terrifying the residents.

The spread of cholera had one beneficial effect. Although how the disease was spread was not understood, it was believed that impure water and lack of sanitation were part of the problem. To counteract this, public health measures began to be introduced throughout North America.

FIVE
The Hazards of Travel by Land

IN SPITE of being so sick, first in Scotland and then in Montreal, Catharine was basically a healthy young woman, and she recovered from cholera surprisingly quickly. In less than two weeks, she and Thomas were able to continue on their way. They headed for her brother Samuel's home on Lake Katchewanooka, part of the Otonabee River system north of Peterborough in Upper Canada. Thomas had been lucky enough to secure a land grant nearby. They planned to learn to live off the land with the help of Sam.

There were few roads in the colony, and those that existed were in poor shape, so people travelled by water as much as possible. For Catharine, used to moderate comfort and completely unfamiliar with the rough ways of this new land, it must have been close to unbearable. Typically this is not the impression she gives her readers in *The Backwoods of Canada*. Her interest in everything around her and her naturally cheerful character helped her to accept the hardships. Commenting that she experienced "a slight sensation of seasickness" while travelling on Lake Ontario, for instance, she continues,

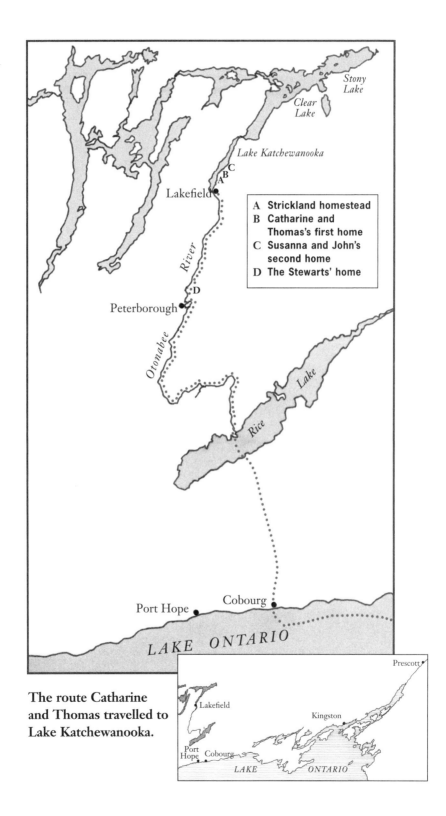

A Strickland homestead
B Catharine and
    Thomas's first home
C Susanna and John's
    second home
D The Stewarts' home

The route Catharine
and Thomas travelled to
Lake Katchewanooka.

"When the waters of the lake are at all agitated, as they sometimes are, by high winds, you might imagine yourself upon a tempest-tossed sea."

In Montreal the Traills were packed into a stagecoach with a family (including four small children with whooping cough) and four large working men who could barely squeeze themselves into the space available. It was a long, hot trip. Catharine described herself as bruised black and blue after the second day. Still, she noted how neat, clean and comfortable the cottages and farms they passed were. The original shanties and log houses had been replaced by pretty frame houses, just as she had described in *The Young Emigrants*. Here she saw no signs of poverty. "Around these habitations," she noted, "were orchards, bending down with a rich harvest of apples, plums, and the American crab, those beautiful little scarlet apples..." As she admired the comfortable farms along the way, she later admitted: "I perhaps overlooked at that time the labour, the difficulties, the privations to which these settlers had been exposed when they first came to this country. I saw it only at a distance of many years, under a high state of cultivation, perhaps in the hands of their children or their children's children, while the toil-worn parent's head was low in the dust."

She saw a number of women spinning in the open air. Hanks of the spun yarn in a rainbow of colours, were hung to dry on the shrubs and fences. Each household, she was told, had a flock of sheep, and the children were taught from a very young age to spin the wool into yarn, dye the yarn and then knit clothes for the family. All of this set Catharine to dreaming about her own future in

THE SPINNING WHEEL

"There is something very picturesque in the great spinning-wheels that are used in this country," Catharine wrote. "The spinster does not sit, but walks to and fro, guiding the yarn with one hand while with the other she turns the wheel."

This illustration is by C.W. Jefferys, famous for the many historical drawings and paintings reproduced in the three-volume *Picture Gallery of Canadian History*. He died in 1952.

her new home, with her husband and children around her.

Obtaining rooms at inns along the way turned out to be a lot less pleasant. When she was led to a closet with a small unprotected bed at one of these, she was horrified. Well, she was told, you can have the room with four beds instead, but the other three beds are taken by the men! She made do with the closet.

At Prescott, on the St. Lawrence, they boarded the largest and best steamer that sailed Lake Ontario, the *Great Britain*. It took them all the way to Cobourg. Catharine enthused about the purple and gold asters and goldenrod they saw along the shore. She was falling in love with the countryside: "I wished to claim all the loveliness for Canada, the country of our adoption and henceforth our home." They reached Cobourg at the end of August. The trip from Montreal had taken them eleven days — a distance that can be travelled in a few hours today.

At Cobourg they headed north from Lake Ontario, travelling in what Catharine called a "light waggon," which was comfortably lined with buffalo robes and pulled by a team of horses. They passed sweeping hills, rolling plains and picturesque woods. But Catharine found the split-rail snake fences "very offensive" to her eyes. She missed the long-established thick, green hedges of England.

As evening fell, they reached Rice Lake and the tavern where they were to spend the night. Here accommodations were worse than ever. "A motley group of immigrants shared the only available room in the loghouse which did duty as a tavern on the shores of Rice

Catharine considered the split-rail fences that she saw along the way to be ugly compared to England's lush, green hedges.

Lake," Catharine remembered in later years. "In a corner, on a buffalo robe spread on the floor, and wrapped in my scotch plaid cloak, I rested my weary limbs. The broad rays of the full moon, streaming in through the panes of the small window, revealed our companions of the Cobourg stage, talking, smoking, or stretched at full length sleeping. On a rude couch at the other end of the room lay a poor sick woman, tossing and turning in a state of feverish unrest, moaning or muttering her delirious fancies, unconscious of the surroundings." If only her family back home in England could have seen Catharine now!

In the morning, they were served fried pork, potatoes and strong tea without any milk. Catharine wasn't tempted to eat very much. Soon they were aboard the steamer that was to take them across Rice Lake and up the Otonabee River. Along the way, Catharine seized any opportunity to step ashore and gather plants and flowers.

Part way to Peterborough, the passengers were to be transferred to a scow, a large, flat-bottomed row boat, capable of navigating the difficult, shallow waters of the river. Unfortunately, long before they reached the meeting point, the steamer ran aground!

Finally, late in the afternoon, the scow appeared, rowed by eight drunken oarsmen, already tired from rowing the extra distance. The travellers and their enormous pile of furniture and supplies were loaded into the boat to a dangerous height, and they continued up the river. The night was beautiful and clear, with brightly shining stars overhead. As darkness fell and the scow neared the rapids, the rowers refused to go any farther until morning. They were still far from Peterborough, and Catharine was terrified that they would have to spend the cold night on an open boat. When one of the other passengers arranged to be rowed to his home across the river, Catharine and Thomas went with him and there hired a young boy to lead them by lantern along a rough trail through the bush to Peterborough. At one point they had to walk over the slippery trunk of a fallen tree to cross a creek. Catharine fell in and got wet to her knees, but recorded this as the first time she had heard the Canadian word "creek."

It was late at night when they arrived at the only inn in Peterborough, only to discover that it was already full. They were tired, wet and cold. Catharine's brother Sam was still a day's journey away. Even the Stewart family, to whom they had a letter of introduction, lived a difficult two hours away. Finally, the kindly innkeeper's wife took pity on Catharine. She knew of the Stewarts and Samuel Strickland and wanted to help. She sat Catharine before the fire, made her a cup of hot tea and gave up her own bed for the Traills. They accepted with gratitude and slept soundly until morning.

"What would my English friends have said could they have seen the room in which my first night in Peterborough was passed? Truly it looked like a bird-cage rather than a bed-chamber. The walls were of lath, unplastered and open so that the cool night breeze blew freshly through the bars and I could see the white frothy water of the rapids of the river dancing in the moonlight as I lay in my bed, and hear the musical ripple as it rushed past the bank on which the house was built."

Six

A Warm Welcome

IT WAS DECIDED that Catharine would remain in Peterborough while Thomas travelled the 10 miles (16 kilometres) to Samuel Strickland's homestead to let him know that his sister was now in the country and ready, along with her new husband, to settle in the same community. Sam had no idea that Catharine and Susanna had married and were on their way to Canada with their husbands. But when Thomas turned up at his door, he was so excited that he insisted on starting at once for Peterborough. In their haste, he and Thomas jumped into a canoe and shot the rapids in the dark (stopping to empty the water out of the canoe three times!). They arrived in Peterborough after Catharine had gone to bed, but she heard her brother's voice and dashed down the stairs for the happy reunion.

The next day, Catharine and Thomas moved on to the home of their acquaintances, the Stewarts, where Catharine stayed for a few days while Thomas continued on to look over their land. Over the next few years Frances Stewart became her closest friend.

Catharine liked Peterborough. It had been settled less

than a decade earlier, but was already a thriving town of about seven hundred. It had saw and grist mills, two inns, stores, a school, a dam, a bridge over the Otonabee, and a farmers' market to which the surrounding settlers brought their goods.

A few days later, the Traills undertook the final stage of the journey to their property, which was near Sam's. They set out in a hired wagon pulled by a span, or pair, of horses. It was loaded with their belongings. Catharine describes the trip in *The Backwoods of Canada*:

There was no palpable road, only a blaze… encumbered by fallen trees, and interrupted by cedar swamps, into which one might sink up to one's knees, unless we took the precaution to step along the trunks of the mossy, decaying logs, or make our footing sure on some friendly block of granite or limestone. What is termed in bush language a "blaze," is nothing more than notches or slices cut off the bark of the trees to mark out the line of the road… our progress was but slow on account of the roughness of the road, which is beset with innumerable obstacles in the shape of loose blocks of limestone, with which the lands on the banks of the river and lakes abound; to say nothing of the fallen trees, big roots, mud-holes, and corduroy bridges over which you go jolt, jolt, jolt, till every bone in your body feels as if it were being dislocated…

Imagine me perched up on a seat composed of carpet-bags, trunks, and sundry packages, in a vehicle little better than a great rough deal box set

Catharine described the "jolt, jolt, jolt" of travelling on "corduroy" roads such as this one, where round logs were placed side by side over muddy or especially rough sections of the road.

on wheels, the sides being merely pegged in so that more than once I found myself in rather an awkward predicament, owing to the said sides falling out. In the very midst of a deep mud-hole out went the front board, and with the shock went the teamster (driver), who looked rather confounded at finding himself lodged just in the middle of a slough.

This drawing of a stagecoach in trouble shows just how difficult travelling could be on early Canadian roads.

The trails followed the Otonabee River when they could, but as evening approached, they could no longer see the river and feared that they were lost and would have to return to Peterborough. They were supposed to meet Sam where the river widened into Lake Katchewanooka, but they couldn't seem to find the right spot. Finally they were surrounded by swamp, and the driver seemed to have lost his way. Exhausted, filthy and giving up hope, they began to retrace their steps. But luck was with them. A small boy appeared on the rough road and told them that they had been going the right way. Back again they went, now in the dark, and soon the lake was before them, gleaming between the trees.

The driver, in a hurry to get on his way, hastily dumped off their belongings. Thomas stood on the shore and called across the lake, hoping that Samuel would hear. They had almost given up hope, when a canoe came gliding across the lake. It was Sam! Soon they were safely across the water enjoying a crackling fire in his cosy log house, describing their experiences to Sam and his wife, Mary, and admiring the three small children – Marie, Robert and Emma.

It had taken them about fifteen days to travel from Montreal to Samuel's home on Lake Katchewanooka.

SEVEN
Making a Home

BY NOW it was fall (another new Canadian word for Catharine), and she and Thomas were welcomed into Samuel's home while they made plans for building a house and clearing some of their land. They were lucky to be able to buy the property between their land and Sam's so that they would be separated from him only by a creek.

Sam's three young children soon became enthusiastic friends of Catharine's. "The children already love me," she wrote. "They have discovered my passion for flowers, which they diligently search for among the stumps and along the lake shore." She was beginning to create what she called her *hortus siccus*, or collection of dried, pressed plants. That autumn Catharine gathered ferns, asters and lichens, giving them all names of her own choosing.

But life in those first few months must have been difficult for everyone. With four adults and three small children, the house was full! Much as Samuel was happy to see his sister and get to know his new brother-in-law, it put a strain on his resources. And although his wife,

Mary, welcomed her two new relatives, it must have upset the family routines. But daily life was hard and the help of the visitors was welcomed. There was no electricity, so most tasks were best done during the daylight hours. There was wood to bring in for the fire. There were lamps to clean as well as the daily washing of dishes. Mending and sewing clothes was a constant task. There was bread to make, and the cooking was all done from scratch. Even the candles and soap were made at home. Families living in the backwoods worked at being as self-sufficient as possible; they bought only what was absolutely necessary. Catharine called it a Robinson Crusoe sort of life.

Typical immigrants on their arrival in Upper Canada.

The roads were still little better than trails, and the Stricklands were some distance from a village where they could get supplies. Orders were relayed with difficulty and were filled only when the next ox-cart was passing their way – a trip that took two days each way. Often the most basic foods were unavailable or arrived in almost ruined condition – "rice, sugar, currants, pepper, and mustard all jumbled into one mess." Potatoes, which all the settlers grew, were sometimes all that saved them from starvation.

The Traills were lucky to start out with a little money to hire help. Certainly Thomas would never have been able to handle the kind of physical work that making a home in the middle of a forest demanded. He hired a number of men – a crew of Irish "choppers" – who moved around the countryside cutting down trees for settlers. They lived in a shanty on the property and cleared three acres (1.2 hectares) of land to be planted the next spring. He and Catharine planned to put in oats, pumpkins, Indian corn and potatoes. The workers also cleared another ten acres (4 hectares) for planting wheat. The tree stumps were left in the ground to rot over the next ten years, creating an ugly landscape that Catharine hated.

The most important job was to build a permanent home. This was begun by making a rectangular box of logs piled one on top of the other. The walls were put up with the help of a work crew of sixteen at a raising bee. "The work went merrily on with the help of plenty of Canadian nectar (whiskey), the honey that our bees are solaced with," wrote Catharine. "Some huge joints of salt pork, a peck [one fourth of a bushel] of potatoes, with rice pudding, and a loaf as big as a Cheshire cheese,

Shanties

In his book, *Twenty-Seven Years in Canada West*, Samuel describes a shanty as a small log building that was higher in the front than in the back. The roof was made by splitting logs in half and hollowing them out. They were then laid side by side, trough side up, running from the front to the back of the shanty. A second row was laid over the first, trough side down, so that no water could run through. A door was cut in the front and, sometimes, one window. The floor was flattened earth.

As soon as sufficient land could be cleared — the most important job — a more substantial frame or stone house would be built.

Most immigrants had to spend the first few months in Canada living in a shanty, which they built as soon as they arrived. Catharine and Thomas were fortunate to be invited to live in her brother Samuel's home for much of this period, since life in a shanty could be wretched.

formed the feast that was to regale them during the raising."

Next beams were installed to support the floor which
was laid with hand-sawn boards, and a door and windows
were cut in the walls. The logs were hewed flat on the
inside, and clay was plastered in the cracks between the
logs. The Traills were able to hire men to do most of this
work, but Thomas glazed the windows himself (something Catharine thought her family back home would
find very amusing). Later verandas, called stoops, would
be added to the front and south sides of the house. When
the pillars of these were wreathed with hops or morning
glories, as was the custom, the stoops would add charm
to the building and provide a cool refuge from the heat
of the summer.

The Importance of Bees

The settlers could not have survived without the help they
gave each other. This cooperation usually took the form of
a bee. There were the raising bees, where neighbours
came together to put up the walls of a house or farm building. There were logging bees and wood-chopping bees for
the men, and quilting bees and corn husking bees for the
women. Any task that could be speeded up with extra
hands might call for a bee. All of them ended in a party
which sometimes got out of hand. Catharine described
bees as "highly useful, and almost indispensable to new
settlers." Her sister Susanna, however, was bitingly critical:
"To me they present the most disgusting picture of a bush
life. They are noisy, riotous, drunken meetings, often ter-
minating in violent quarrels, sometimes even in blood-
shed."

By Christmas of 1833, the Traills were in their new log house. They had a living room, bedroom, kitchen and pantry, and above was an open second floor with room for three more bedrooms. This was a rough dwelling compared to what they had known in England. "We do not, however, lack comfort in our humble home," Catharine wrote to her family, "although it is not exactly such as we could wish, it is as good as, under the circumstances, we could expect to obtain."

Eight
Settling In

THE FIRST WINTER the Traills spent in their new home was unusually mild until February. Then, for days at a time, it was so cold that it was impossible to keep the house warm. Water inside the house was frozen when they got up in the mornings and, with no running water or indoor toilet, it was a cold journey to the outhouse! As Catharine described it, "The sensation of cold early in the morning was very painful, producing an involuntary shuddering, and an almost convulsive feeling in the chest." The ground was covered with deep snow until the middle of March. By early May, however, a rapid change in temperature made the heat unbearable. The black flies and mosquitoes were even worse. One solution was to have little smouldering piles of wood chips inside the house to drive the insects out. This was almost as uncomfortable for the humans as for the insects!

Catharine may have found the May heat particularly hard to bear because she was about to have her first child. Baby James was born in June. Taking care of a baby was a time-consuming job in the backwoods of the

Catharine wrote about enjoying her early experiences on the frozen lake (identifying Samuel only by his initial):

> Soon after this I made another excursion on the ice, but it was not in quite so sound a state. We nevertheless walked on for about three-quarters of a mile. We were overtaken on our return by S– with a hand sleigh, which is a sort of wheelbarrow, such as porters use, without sides, and instead of a wheel, is fixed on wooden runners, which you can drag over the snow and ice with the greatest ease, if ever so heavily laden. S– insisted that he would draw me home over the ice like a Lapland lady on a sledge. I was soon seated in state, and in another minute felt myself impelled forward with a velocity that nearly took away my breath. By the time we reached the shore I was in a glow from head to foot.

early nineteenth century. The diapers and all other clothing had to be made and washed by hand. There was no ready-made formula or baby food. In the winter, there was little choice in what the baby (or the adults) had to eat. No green vegetables, only root crops that could be stored, such as potatoes, carrots and turnips. There was no fruit, either, except for dried apples, and even these were hard to come by in the early years. In spite of all this, James was a healthy little boy and, in a letter to her mother back in England, Catharine described him as "fat and lively" and "the pride and delight of his foolish mother's heart."

All summer the work of clearing the land continued. The trees had been cut down during the winter, but the job of clearing and burning the brush remained to be

Clearing the land in the 1830s.

done before the ground could be planted. After the large timbers had been trimmed, cut into lengths and piled together, first the brush and then the logs were burned. The woods were dense and almost impenetrable all around them. "When the Backwoodsman first beholds the dense mass of dark forest which his hands must clear from the face of the ground," wrote Catharine, "he sees in it nothing more than a wilderness of vegetation which it is his lot to destroy: he does not know then how much that is essential to the comfort of his household is contained in the wild forest." But after the clearing, there still remained large areas of forest to supply the settlers with wood for the stove, and from which they made furniture, tool handles, shingles and other essential items.

The burnings could be dangerous. There was always the possibility that fire could spread to the surrounding forest. "It is, however," wrote Catharine, "a magnificent sight to see the blazing trees and watch the awful progress of the conflagration, as it hurries onward, consuming all before it..."

That summer the Traills grew wheat, rye, oats, potatoes and corn around the stumps. Their aim was to make themselves as self-sufficient as possible so that very little food, for themselves or the animals, would have to be bought and paid for with Thomas's meagre half-pay income. Their only tools were a spade, a couple of hoes, several axes, two reaping hooks, and "a queer sort of harrow... made in the shape of a triangle for the better passing between the stumps."

By fall they had two oxen, two cows, two calves, three pigs, ten hens, three ducks, and what Catharine described as "a pretty brown pony." But because the pony was such a skillful fence-jumper (she could clear seven rails) they had to sell her.

Catharine had enthusiastic plans for a garden at the front of the house that year but, with a new baby to care for and so many things she had still to learn as a pioneer homemaker, she was able to accomplish much less than she had hoped. Cooking and preserving were among her most important tasks. Many of the foods were new to her: Indian corn, so important in pioneer households; pumpkins ("there is not a better dish eaten than a good pumpkin-pie"); apples used dried, preserved, jellied, as apple butter or sauce, and especially as cider, one of the most important backwoods drinks. Even bread was made differently in Canada; Catharine advocated using hops as "rising" or yeast. Wild fruit and berries were gathered in

Making Maple Syrup

One of the first and most valuable things the early settlers learned from the Native people was how to obtain syrup (Catharine called it molasses) and sugar from maple trees. They made excellent substitutes for cane sugar, which had to be imported and was expensive.

In the spring, when the temperature rose above freezing during the day and dropped below at night, the trees could be tapped: "The first thing to be done in tapping the maples is to provide little rough troughs to catch the sap as it flows: these are merely pieces of pine-tree, hollowed with the axe. The tapping of the tree is done by cutting a gash in  the bark, or boring a hole with an auger…. A slightly-hollowed piece of cedar or elder is then inserted, so as to slant downwards and direct the sap into the trough."

All day sap was collected and poured into a large iron kettle. In the evening, as the sap slowed, an open fire was lit and the kettle hung over it from two tripods. "It was a pretty and picturesque sight to see the sugar-boilers, with their bright log-fire among the trees, now stirring up the blazing pile, now throwing in the liquid and stirring it down with a big ladle. When the fire grew fierce, it boiled and foamed up in the kettle, and they had to throw in fresh sap to keep it from running over."

When the sap had turned to syrup, some of it was transferred to pots to be boiled further into sugar. Catharine supervised this stage during her first spring in Canada. She was proud of her success with the sugar, and they were able to produce three gallons of syrup as well. The latter "proved a great comfort to us," she wrote, "forming a nice ingredient in cakes and an excellent sauce for puddings."

season and preserved for the winter. She had dreams of cultivating native fruits — strawberries, raspberries, currants, grapes, cherries, plums and gooseberries — in her own garden. This, too, would have to wait for another year.

For Susanna and John Moodie, the first year in the new country was not nearly as pleasant. They arrived only a week or so behind Catharine and Thomas, but instead of travelling on to join the rest of the family, they bought land just west of Cobourg. Everything seemed to go wrong and Susanna, in her witty, satirical style, describes it in detail in her famous book, *Roughing It in the Bush*: "The next night we slept in the new house, a demon of unrest had taken possession of it in the shape of a countless swarm of mice. They scampered over our pillows, and jumped upon our faces, squeaking and cutting a thousand capers over the floor." Early in 1834 they pulled up stakes again and took up a land grant next to the Traills' property. Susanna now had a two-year-old and a baby, and Catharine's James was eight months old. The Moodies moved in with Catharine and Thomas, and John began to supervise the building of their new home.

It was a difficult time for the two families. "In spite of my sister's kindness and hospitality," wrote Susanna, "I longed to find myself once more settled in a home of my own." By late spring the Moodies had moved into a comfortable, two-storey log house that Susanna described as "a palace when compared to... the miserable cabin we had wintered in during the severe winter of 1833."

For almost six years, the two sisters lived along the shore of Lake Katchewanooka within walking distance of each other and close to their brother. Although it was a hard life, for which they were little prepared, they could count on each other through the bad times.

NINE
Life in the Backwoods

OVER THE NEXT six years, Catharine and Susanna lived as neighbours in the bush, and their families continued to grow. By 1838 each had four children. The children played with homemade wooden whistles and dolls, wound balls of string for catch and played games such as hide-and-seek. At an early age they would help with the chores – collecting eggs, cleaning boots, picking berries, plucking feathers for beds and taking care of the younger children.

The work pioneer women had to do is difficult for us to imagine, although the book that Catharine wrote after living in Canada for twenty years gives us some idea. *The Canadian Settler's Guide* was written to help new immigrant women prepare for life as pioneers. In it she gives practical advice on the many things they would have to learn. She describes how to furnish a house with little money, suggesting that "A delightful easy chair can be made out of a very rough material – nothing better than a common flour barrel," and describes how to stuff a mattress with corn husks. She talks about the importance of a garden, especially an orchard, saying that all the ladies along the Otonabee River care for their orchards themselves, and grow their own vegetables and flowers too. She emphasizes the value of trees for building houses, barns and fences, for firewood, and for the ashes used in making soap. She includes recipes for making candles, for tea and coffee substitutes from hemlock twigs and dandelion roots, for butter and for cheese, and gives all kinds of other pioneer recipes for wild berries, fish and game. She has instructions for curing meat so it can be stored. She describes which plants to use for dyeing cloth and reminds readers that they will have to be prepared to make most of the family's clothes.

"It depends upon ourselves to better our own condition," she wrote, "cheerfulness of mind and activity of body are essential to the prosperity of the household."

For Catharine it was particularly important to remain cheerful, since Thomas was completely unsuited to the rough pioneer life. The heavy outdoor work in the fields and with the animals was totally new to him. He was studious by nature and attracted to a more contemplative life, and he was not as resilient as Catharine. From time to time he was deeply depressed. Although Catharine, who was either pregnant or nursing a baby much of the time during these years, must often have been tired and worried, she kept these feelings to herself except in letters to her closest friends and to Susanna. She loved her children dearly, and her fascination with the natural world around her was a comfort, as was her affection for Thomas, which never diminished. Her religious beliefs, which were central to her life, helped her to face the daily ordeals.

Susanna's life was at least as difficult, and she found it

Visit to a Wigwam

During these years Catharine was able to get to know some of the Native Chippewa. She writes about visiting one family in the winter and describes their birchbark home:

[It] is first formed with light poles, planted round so as to enclose a circle of ten or twelve feet in diameter; between these poles are drawn large sheets of birch-bark both within and without, leaving an opening of bare poles at the top so as to form an outlet for the smoke; the outer walls are also banked with snow, so as to exclude the air entirely from beneath....

I was at a loss to conceive where the Indians kept their stores, clothes and other moveables, the wigwam being so small that there seemed no room for anything besides themselves and their hounds. Their ingenuity, however, supplied the want of room, and I soon discovered a plan that answered all the purposes of closets, bags, boxes, etc., the inner lining of birch-bark being drawn between the poles so as to form hollow pouches all round; in these pouches were stored their goods.

harder to bear. She had not wanted to leave London, and her early impressions of Upper Canada come through starkly in the final words of her book *Roughing It in the Bush*: "If these sketches should prove the means of deterring one family from sinking their property, and shipwrecking all their hopes, by going to reside in the backwoods of Canada, I shall consider myself amply repaid for revealing the secrets of the prison-house, and feel that I have not toiled and suffered in the wilderness in vain."

In 1837, the whole family, particularly the Moodies, were shaken by a political uprising in Upper Canada. Samuel, Thomas and John were all members of the local militia, and when rebellion broke out in December of that year, they rushed to support the government. "The tidings of the rising was brought to our clearing from Peterborough," Catharine wrote, "the messenger arriving at midnight through the snow to call all loyal men to the defence of their country. No time was lost that night, and before dawn I said farewell to my husband."

It was over before the men arrived but, unlike Samuel and Thomas, who returned home immediately, John Moodie stayed on. The pay he received as an officer was important for the family, but Susanna missed her husband, whom she loved deeply, and she had to manage the farm and care for the children alone. Only the help of the Traills and Sam made it possible and, although her life was agonizing for the next two years, she bore it with courage. When Catharine and Thomas left the neighbourhood that spring, life became even harder. "They have been months of sickness anxiety and sorrow," she wrote to John in March of 1839, "and worse than all, of

The Rebellion of 1837

In Upper Canada, discontent between the group of men in control of the government (referred to as the Family Compact) and those in the reform movement (under the leadership of William Lyon Mackenzie) led to a violent confrontation. The Family Compact had influence over almost everything in the colony, from land grants to education, and favoured business in their decisions. The reformers, many of them new immigrants from the United States, wanted a more democratic form of government that took into account the interests of the farming settlers. They gathered at Montgomery's tavern north of Toronto and marched down Yonge Street. There they were met by a group of militia and volunteers loyal to the Family Compact, most of them British immigrants like the Stricklands, Traills and Moodies. Two rebels and one loyalist lost their lives in the following short battle that was fought with rifles, staves and pitchforks. Mackenzie and most of his men fled to the United States, but two of his supporters were hanged.

Although the reformers were defeated, British Loyalists like Catharine gradually came to support a movement towards more responsible government. By the end of the 1840s, this had been achieved under the more moderate leadership of Robert Baldwin.

absence from you." On New Year's day of 1840, Susanna and the children were finally able to join John in Belleville, where he had been appointed sheriff.

Life now became easier for Susanna and, in spite of her earlier warnings about the horrors of life in Canada, she came to love the country. In later years she wrote: "The sorrows and trials that I experienced during my first eight years' residence in Canada, have been more than counterbalanced by the remaining twelve of comfort and peace. I have long felt the deepest interest in her prosperity and improvement. I no longer regard myself as an alien on her shores, but her daughter by adoption, — the happy mother of Canadian children, — rejoicing in the warmth and hospitality of a Canadian Home."

TEN
Poverty, Hunger and Fire

L IFE IN THE BACKWOODS gradually improved as more settlers moved into the area. A road was constructed, and people no longer had to cross the lake in a canoe to pick up supplies from Peterborough. In spite of this, however, life grew increasingly difficult for the Traills. They were trying to sell their property so they could move closer to civilization like Susanna and John, who were now living in Belleville. Early in 1839, Catharine and Thomas, now with four children under six years of age (James, Kate, Harry and Annie), finally found a buyer for their property, but the sale didn't even leave them enough to pay their debts. Thomas tried to get administrative work in the army or the government, but without success. They tried everything to make a living. Thomas worked in the orchard. Catharine grew vegetables and her beloved flowers. She tried to start a school for young children, but it was too much for her. In 1840 she had a baby girl who died within the year. Another girl was born in 1841 and her seventh child, born in 1843, died as an infant. Nothing seemed to allow them to get ahead, and Thomas's small yearly income wasn't enough for them to live on. Even though *The Backwoods of Canada* was a huge success in England, Catharine received very little in the way of payment. In 1842 she wrote to the publisher, "...you will perhaps learn with regret that while her little volume is read with pleasure by the talented and the wealthy, the writer and her infant family now increased by five helpless children, is struggling with poverty and oppressed by many cares."

For years they moved from one rented house to another, all in the Peterborough area. Finally they faced destitution and were able to survive only with the help of friends and neighbours, and with the packages of clothing, housewares, reading material and sewing supplies that continued to arrive from England.

Another child, William, was born in 1844. In a letter to Susanna, Catharine wrote, "My dear husband was fretting himself to death and me too, for both my health and spirits were sinking under the load of mental anxiety more on his account than the circumstances, and want of strengthening diet — bread, a few potatoes, given us by dear good Mr Stewart, and a few fishes from day to day and week to week have been our fare the dear children eat it with single and contented hearts but baby and I grow thin."

Thomas was unable to cope with the extent of their financial problems, or even to discuss them with Catharine. At one point, she wrote to John Moodie, "Can the bailiffs seize the flour and pork that are in the house?"

In 1846 they moved to a house on the south shore of Rice Lake that had been lent to them by a friend. Catharine missed the many friends they had to leave

behind, especially Frances Stewart, who shared her love
of literature and botany. They compared the plant specimens they collected, and both were deeply religious.
When they were not living close enough to visit, the two
friends corresponded frequently. Finding another like-
minded neighbour in the sparsely settled country was
not likely.

Catharine's last child, Walter, was born in 1848. By
then she had had eight children, six still living. It was not
unusual for babies or young children to die at that time.
Catharine was sick herself much of the time, probably
from the combined strain of childbearing, fatigue and
lack of a proper diet. When food was short, her husband
and the children came first.

All the settlers suffered from a variety of infections,
irritations and diseases. Catharine and Susanna must
have found it comforting to be able to write to each
other about their suffering, which they did frequently.
The letters between the two are full of accounts of dis-
abling tumours, lumbago, aching joints, painful teeth,
coughs, stomach troubles and infections of the eyes and
throat. Catharine wrote, in 1854, "I have been wanting
this week past to write to you… but have been suffering
so much with one ailment or another that I could not."

In those days there was little help for doctors attempt-
ing to diagnose a patient – no x-rays, no blood tests and
few effective drugs aside from aspirin and morphine.
The Natives taught them much about home remedies.
Flax seeds under the eyelid or a tea bath helped when
something got into an eye. Skunk cabbage was boiled for
asthma. Cloves, opium or cayenne were recommended
for toothache. Little was known then about the causes of

In the nineteenth century, paper was often hard to come by. For this reason, every scrap was used and letters were often "cross written." The page was written on one way, then turned and written on again, so that twice as much could be fitted on the sheet. In this letter, Susanna is writing to "My dearest Catherine." (Even Catharine's own family sometimes spelled her name with an e. In her books, however, and on other official documents such as her will, it was always spelled Catharine.)

infection, and antibiotics to kill disease-causing bacteria would not become available for nearly a hundred years; patients either recovered on their own or died. Women frequently died in childbirth, as did their infants. Minor irritations such as indigestion, warts, boils and cankers were widespread. Problems related to the heart, blood pressure, and such diseases as diabetes and polio were untreatable. Mental illness was a mystery.

Settlers in the backwoods learned to handle medical crises by themselves. Samuel, Catharine's brother, acted as dentist for the community, which usually meant pulling painfully diseased teeth. Many of the settlers were toothless in their later years. Catharine was often called upon to be a midwife when a child was to be born. When John Moodie broke a leg he fashioned his own makeshift cast. Everyone helped out in times of sickness.

The settlers were dependent on each other for many things. Mail, the only way to keep in touch with friends and family, was carried by whoever was travelling. Horses, carts and tools were lent freely. And gifts of wood or food were often all that saved the lives of those in need.

Finally, in 1848, the Traills were able to buy Oaklands, a property south of Rice Lake, with money Thomas received by cashing in his half-pay officer's income. Sam and other friendly neighbours guaranteed the mortgage.

Throughout her life, Catharine continued to write. Writing was important to her, and she was always trying to add to the family's meagre income. *The Backwoods of Canada* was frequently reprinted, and her articles and stories about plant and animal life appeared in many journals in England, the United States and Canada. In 1852, her novel about three children lost in the wilderness, *Canadian Crusoes: A Tale of the Rice Lake Plains*, was an immediate success. The financial rewards, however, remained slight; often she received little or no payment for her work.

On August 25, 1857, Catharine awoke in a panic. The

Lost in the Woods!

Catharine was fascinated by stories she heard of children being lost in the woods, and sometimes never again found. In her novel *Canadian Crusoes*, three teenagers – Catharine, her brother Hector, and their cousin Louis – are lost in what was then dense bush south of Rice Lake. In this short excerpt, the three have just survived their first night. It would be three long, adventurous years before they found their way back home.

"Be not cast down, Catharine," said her brother, cheeringly; "we may not be so far from home as you think. As soon as you are rested we will set out again, and we may find something to eat; there must be strawberries on these sunny banks."

Catharine soon yielded to the voice of her brother, and drying her eyes, proceeded to descend the sides of the steep valley that lay to one side of the high ground where they had been sitting.

Suddenly darting down the bank, she exclaimed, "Come, Hector; come Louis: here indeed is provision to keep us from starving;" – for her eye had caught the bright red strawberries among the flowers and herbage on the slope; large ripe strawberries, the very finest she had ever seen.

house was filled with smoke. She shook Thomas awake and they dashed to rescue the children. They knew that the old log house would soon be up in flames. They did their best to save whatever else they could, but the fire spread rapidly in the dry wood of the house and they were left with almost nothing. All the family papers, their precious journals, the personal letters from friends and family, and all the things they had collected over the years were lost. Catharine was able to save only her botanical studies, but she was grateful for that. They would be the basis of a future book.

Catharine seems not to have recorded her feelings during this difficult time (how would she have found the time?), but Thomas wrote a short note in his journal: "At three o'clock Mrs T awoke me, saying the house was on fire. I had barely time to awake the sleepers upstairs, and we got out a part of our bedding, wearing apparell a few of our books, 3 chairs and 3 tables before the whole house was in a blaze. I am so thankful that all our lives were saved, particularly our dear Walter, whose room was full of smoke when he was called, that I hardly regret what was lost. Thanks to God for all his mercies."

Fire was the scourge of early settlements. Most houses were made of wood. They were heated by stoves or fireplaces that were often dangerous, with poor chimneys. There were no fire stations, and often no readily available water. Neighbours were always quick to respond to fight the blaze, but often, as in the case of the Traills, there was just no time. In villages, the fear was always that the whole community would go up in smoke.

Gifts of clothing, furniture and money flowed in.

Friends and relatives knew that they might be next to need help. The family scattered to live with others for the next two years. The children were now grown, or growing up. James was married with a home of his own. The two youngest children – William, thirteen, and Walter, nine – went to stay with him. Kate and Annie, twenty-one and nineteen, went to one friend; Mary, sixteen, to another; and Harry to a third. Thomas and Catharine were taken in by Sam.

The loss of their home and belongings was the final

Catharine in her mourning clothes after the death of Thomas.

Catharine always wrote respectfully of Thomas. Others, however, sometimes saw him differently. A visitor from Scotland described him as "a tall thin faced man of about fifty with a kind of loose great coat of grey cloth a good deal faded and stained ... a nose very much stained with snuff, hands and face evidently in want of soap and water yet with all this unprepossessing exterior evidently a kind hearted and well informed man."

blow for Thomas. He fell into a deep depression from which he never recovered, and died less than two years after the fire.

Unlike Susanna's, Catharine's was not a passionate marriage, but she never regretted her decision to marry Thomas. In her journal, after his death, she wrote: "With some foreign eccentricities of manner, and some faults of nervous irritability of constitution, he was a true hearted loyal gentleman, faithful in deed and word — a kind and benevolent disposition, a loving father, husband and friend — a scholar and a true gentleman, whose virtues will be remembered long after his faults have been forgotten."

She wore black for fifteen years after his death, as a sign of respect and mourning.

Eleven
Botanizing

T HE FIRE, the scattering of the family and the death of her husband brought enormous changes for Catharine. In 1860 she was fifty-eight years old. James and Annie were married and had homes of their own. Katie was twenty-four, still at home and devoting her life to her mother and the family. Harry was twenty-three; he had been responsible for much of the farm work before the fire and was now working in lumber shanties in the winter and on farms in the summer. Mary was twenty and had begun to teach school in Lakefield in order to contribute to the family income. Will and Walter were still boys, only sixteen and twelve.

The older children, growing up in the backwoods, had received little or no formal education, except what they had been taught at home, which was probably considerable. Catharine had planned to start a school at one time, and with her own background she would certainly have ensured that the children received at least the basics. They had managed to make their way in the world — even, in Mary's case, as a teacher — but Catharine was determined that the younger two would have a better start. The immediate problem, however, was to find a place to live.

As always, friends and family were prepared to help as much as they could. Financial gifts arrived from friends and from her sister Agnes, who had been exceedingly successful with her biographies of English royalty. ("Your good generous Aunt Agnes," Catharine wrote to her daughter Mary, "sent me a bill for £20 and with this sum I have purchased a lovely bit of ground… it has some charming trees that will make it most ornamental when laid out.") She also received a significant grant from a British fund for her valuable contribution to the settlement of Canada through her book *The Canadian Settler's Guide*. With the help of Sam a house was built for her on the shores of the Otonabee in the now thriving village of Lakefield, and in 1862, Catharine, Mary, Kate and the two boys moved into their new home. They named the house Westove in honour of the Traill estate in the Orkneys.

Money continued to be a problem. Sometimes the house would be rented for a time, while Catharine and the children lived with her daughter Mary and her young family to save a few dollars. Always Catharine continued to write and sell her stories, and to study and collect plants from the wild. Catharine's life in the decades after Thomas's death, however, gradually became more comfortable. She never had much money and often had to just scrape by, but the extreme poverty of her earlier decades in Canada was past. Catharine was basically healthy and enjoyed the love of a close-knit family. She faced the many painful episodes in her life bravely and then put them behind her. "I think that I have a happy

CATHARINE PARR TRAILL
1802 - 1899
A member of the literary Strickland family, this talented author married Lieut. Thomas Traill and emigrated to Upper Canada 1832. For seven years they struggled unsuccessfully to establish a profitable farm on bushland in Douro Township Subsequently, they lived at Ashburnham and Rice Lake. In 1862, following her husband's death, Mrs. Traill's daughters purchased Westove and she lived here the rest of her life. Her best known book, "The Backwoods of Canada", is based on her pioneering experiences. In her Studies of Plant Life in Canada and other works she proved herself a gifted botanist.
Erected by the Ontario Archaeological and Historic Sites Board.

faculty of forgetting past sorrows and only remembering the pleasures," she wrote. Her religious convictions continued to give her strength.

By the 1870s there were three "Kates" living together in Westove. When Harry, who had taken a job as a guard at the Kingston Penitentiary, was killed by two of the convicts, he left his wife Lily with three small children. In order to help the young widow, Catharine and her eldest daughter, Kate, took responsibility for Harry's daughter Katie (sometimes known as Katie 3!). Catharine's daughter Mary died in 1892 at the age of fifty-one, seven years before Catharine, but Kate, Annie and Will all survived into the twentieth century.

Catharine's "botanizing" (the popular term for collecting, identifying and mounting plants) was praised both in Canada and in England. Today she is frequently referred to as one of the country's early botanists, a description she always denied, believing that she was just someone who loved to collect plants and write about them. But her supporters, such as James Fletcher, the first botanist at the Central Experimental Farm in Ottawa, disagreed. "With regard to your disclaiming the title of botanist," he wrote, "all I can say is, I wish a fraction of one percent of the students of plants who call themselves botanists, could use their eyes half as well as you have done." Her articles had a poetic quality no longer found in scientific descriptions, and they convey the pleasure she found in plant life: "Well worth seeing, indeed, is a bed of pitcher plants, especially in the month

Westove, the house built for Catharine in Lakefield in the 1860s. This plaque now stands at the entrance to the property.

Aspidium marginale var. *Traillae*, Mrs. Traill's shield fern, as collected and mounted by her at Stony Lake in 1893. Dr. George Lawson of Queen's University had it named in her honour.

of June, their flowering time. The tall, naked scape bears one large deep red blossom. From the globular five-rayed ovary rises a short, pillar-like style which expands into a thin yellow umbrella-shaped body, elegantly scalloped at the edges and covering the floral organs, adding greatly to the beauty of the flower."

Susanna's daughter Agnes Fitzgibbon had become a talented artist. In 1867, she and Catharine created a book, *Canadian Wild Flowers*, with drawings by Agnes and plant descriptions by Catharine. In the original edition the pictures were printed and then individually hand-coloured by the artist. The large-format publication was a beautiful and unusual undertaking in nineteenth-century Canada. It was a publishing success — in part due to Agnes's contacts in society — and was reprinted a number of times.

Throughout the rest of her life, Catharine continued to collect plants and flowers, to dry them by pressing them between sheets of paper, and then mounting them in albums, carefully identifying each. No matter how confined and poor she might be, this was something she could do in spare moments, without special equipment. The only problem was finding the paper she needed. She often sent the albums and mountings as gifts to others in the field with whom she kept in close touch, but she was also able to sell them and thus add to the household income.

In 1885 her major botanical work, *Studies of Plant Life in Canada*, was published. "It is not a book for the learned," she wrote. "The aim of the writer is simply to show the real pleasure that may be obtained from a habit of observing what is offered to the eye of the traveller."

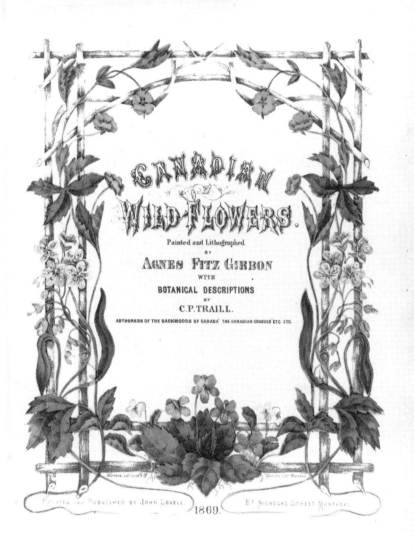

The large-format book by Catharine, with hand-coloured
illustrations by her niece Agnes Fitzgibbon.

Catharine was eighty-three years old. Even in her nineties she could be found out on the rocky trails and rolling hills near her home looking for new plants. A journalist wrote of visiting Catharine at her cottage on Minne-wa-wa Island when she was ninety-one: "There the aged naturalist was in her element, clambering perilously over the rocks and peering into hidden nooks in search of specimens of flowers and lichens, hoarding her newfound treasures as a miner his gold."

Epilogue

CATHARINE PARR TRAILL died on August 29, 1899, still writing at ninety-seven years of age. She had lived through almost the whole of the nineteenth century, and she left behind an extraordinary legacy.

As a naturalist Catharine was eager to learn about everything in the world around her. Although plants were closest to her heart, she studied birds, animals, rocks and fossils. Her studies of plant life included not only the wildflowers that she loved so well, but the ferns, mosses, lichens and many species of grasses she found around her home. She exchanged pressed plants with other naturalists and friends around the world and amassed a notable collection that still survives in archives and museums throughout the country.

As a writer she has told us more about the life of a pioneer in nineteenth-century Ontario than anyone else, including the kinds of personal details that few others considered worth recording. Her fiction, although very popular in her own time, is written in a style no longer appealing to readers, but her descriptions of the back-

Catharine with two of her granddaughters, in a picture taken during her last summer, on the porch of the cottage at Minne-wa-wa Island. Her granddaughters used to complain that everyone was so charmed by Catharine that they didn't stand a chance with their own boyfriends when she was around!

woods and of the difficulties she and her family faced will never lose their interest.

Catharine received a number of tributes in her own lifetime, in addition to having the shield fern named for

An Extraordinary Literary Family

The writings of the three Stricklands who made their homes in southern Ontario in the nineteenth century give us a rich and varied picture of life in their times. Samuel, although not primarily a writer, was the author of *Twenty-Seven Years in Canada West*, a book that describes his experiences as a pioneer and provides practical information for others. Susanna, particularly in her anecdotal descriptions of the unforgettable characters in *Roughing It in the Bush*, has amused and intrigued generations with her wry, sharp-witted style (and has been the inspiration for many later writers). And Catharine, in a more practical fashion, revealed just how these new Canadians were able to survive a way of life more difficult than we can easily imagine.

Their memories are honoured in this plaque that stands on the banks of the Otonabee River in Lakefield, not far from where Catharine spent the last decades of her life.

her. Her work was recognized by historical societies in Toronto and Peterborough. The Royal Literary Fund in England awarded her a small pension in recognition of her contributions as a writer. One of her friends in Canada, Sir Sanford Fleming, organized a testimonial in her honour that included a gift of $1,000, a considerable sum for the time. In 1893 she was granted ownership of a small island near her home, Polly Cow's Island, which she wished preserved for the sake of the grave of a Native girl buried there and, in connection with this, she received a letter from Ottawa that read in part: "It has been a great pleasure to everyone here, from the highest to the lowest official, to do everything in their power to do you honourable service… for your lifelong devotion to Canada."

In spite of this, Catharine would be astonished to learn that people still read her books, still treasure her descriptions of flowers and plants, and are still fascinated by the hundreds of letters she wrote (published in the book *I Bless You in My Heart*). She would also be very pleased to know of the respect with which she is remembered.

Glossary

amber: Fossilized tree sap, used for the making of jewellery and ornaments.

bleeding: The taking of blood from a sick person, sometimes using leeches. It was believed that this would help the body heal itself.

botany: The study of plants.

cholera: An infectious disease caused by bacteria, often fatal.

deal box: A box made of rough wooden planks.

draughts: A board game, also known as checkers.

emigrant: One who leaves one's country to move to another.

epidemic: A situation where an infectious disease spreads quickly through a community.

gout: A disease causing pain and inflammation in small joints, often of the big toe.

grist mill: A mill that crushes grist, i.e., corn or other grain.

guinea: A British gold coin, no longer in use, worth twenty-one shillings in the currency of the time.

harrow: A kind of cultivator for breaking up the soil or weeding.

lath: A thin strip of wood.

linseywoolsey: A fabric woven out of coarse wool and cotton.

lumbago: Rheumatic pains in the lower back.

pelisse: An ankle-length cloak with or without sleeves.

quarantine: To separate or confine people with an infectious disease.

quill pen: A pen made from the hollow stem of a feather.

Robinson Crusoe: The hero of a famous eighteenth-century novel written by Daniel Defoe, about a man cast away on a desert island.

slough: A swamp or small, marshy pond or lake.

smallpox: A contagious disease caused by a virus, character-
ized by fever and painful blisters called pox, often fatal.

snake fence: A fence made of rails overlapped in a zig-zag
pattern.

staves: The plural of staff, a stick or pole used for walking
or for a weapon.

tax-cart: An open cart, often used for trade, on which little
or no tax needed to be paid.

typhoid: A contagious disease caused by bacterial infection
with fever, a red rash and severe stomach upset; often
fatal.

Suggestions for Further Reading

Both Catharine Parr Traill and her sister, Susanna Moodie, wrote and published widely during their lifetimes. A number of their books continue to be available. These are some of them and books by others that tell more about Catharine's life:

The Backwoods of Canada by Catharine Parr Traill. Toronto: McClelland & Stewart, reprinted 1989.
   Catharine's account of her experiences as she travelled to Canada, and a record of her early years as a pioneer. One of the best personal records of what life was like for the early settlers.

I Bless You in My Heart: Selected Correspondence of Catharine Parr Traill, edited by Carl Ballstadt, Elizabeth Hopkins, and Michael A. Peterman. Toronto: University of Toronto Press, 1996.
   A collection of more than a hundred letters written by Catharine to family and friends over a seventy-year period, from 1830 to 1899. They tell modern readers much about the joys and sorrows of nineteenth-century immigrant life.

Pearls & Pebbles by Catharine Parr Traill, edited by Elizabeth Thompson. Toronto: Natural Heritage Books, 1999.
   A collection of essays by Catharine, including memories of her childhood and essays on the plants and animals near her home in Upper Canada.

Roughing It in the Bush by Susanna Moodie. Toronto: McClelland & Stewart, reprinted 1989.
   Susanna's account of her experiences as a settler, often bitter, frequently humorous, always lively. She saw life with a more critical eye than Catharine. A book considered to be a classic of pioneer literature.

Sisters in the Wilderness: The Lives of Susanna Moodie and Catharine Parr Traill by Charlotte Gray. Toronto: Viking, 1999.
A full-length biography of the two sisters. This is a lively, readable account of the life and times of Catharine and Susanna.

PICTURE CREDITS

Cover image: Toronto Reference Library/T-14381; frontispiece and page 17 (left): National Archives of Canada/C-067337; 11: National Archives of Canada/PA-202944; 17 (right): National Library of Canada/NL-15658; 26: C.P. Traill, *The Young Emigrants; or, Pictures of Canada*/National Archives of Canada/C-149539; 29: R.E. Merrick/Maritime Museum of the Atlantic/MP4.11.1 N#1016; 32: *Canadian Illustrated News*/National Archives of Canada/C-062719; 36: C.W. Jefferys, *The Picture Gallery of Canadian History*/National Library of Canada/NL-22482; 38: Carol Martin; 43: Toronto Reference Library/T-14377; 44: C.W. Jefferys, *The Picture Gallery of Canadian History*/National Library of Canada/NL-22484; 47: C.W. Jefferys, *The Picture Gallery of Canadian History*/National Library of Canada/NL-22486; 49: Toronto Reference Library/T-14381; 54: C.W. Jefferys, *The Picture Gallery of Canadian History*/National Library of Canada/NL-22485; 56: C.W. Jefferys, *The Picture Gallery of Canadian History*/National Library of Canada/NL- 22487; 61: *Canadian Illustrated News*/National Archives of Canada/C-050301; 63: C.W. Jefferys, *The Picture Gallery of Canadian History*/National Library of Canada/NL-22483; 68: National Archives of Canada/C-149603; 72: Peterborough Centennial Museum and Archives/112.72.10; 76 (top): National Archives of Canada/C067354; 76 (bottom): Michael Solomon; 78: Queen's University Library, WD Jordan Special Collections – Lorne Pierce; 80: Agnes FitzGibbon and C.P. Traill, *Canadian Wild Flowers*; 83: Peterborough Centennial Museum and Archives/PG1-13; 84: Michael Solomon.

Acknowledgements

Most of the information in this book comes from the many writings of Catharine Parr Traill herself, and from those of others in her family.

I am grateful to my friend, and esteemed writer, Janet Lunn, for her comments on the manuscript, and to my editor, Shelley Tanaka, for her insightful questions and comments. I would also like to thank my daughter, Pamela Martin, for encouragement and assistance along the way. My brother, Donald Wood, gave me a place to stay while researching in the Peterborough area, and supplied additional information from that region.

Libraries and archives are essential to the research involved in a biographical work of this kind; the National Archives of Canada (special thanks to Anne Goddard), the National Library of Canada, the Edith & Lorne Pierce Canadiana Collection at Queen's University, the Peterborough Centennial Museum and Historical Archives, the Trent University Archives and Special Collections, and the Belleville Public Library were all particularly helpful.

A grant from the Ontario Arts Council helped me to complete the writing, and I am grateful for their assistance.

INDEX

CAROL MARTIN is a writer, consultant and exhibition curator with a keen interest in the fascinating stories and individuals in Canadian history. Her previous books include *Martha Black: Gold Rush Pioneer* and *A History of Canadian Gardening*. She lives in southeastern Ontario in the hamlet of Thomasburg, north of Belleville — not far from Catharine Parr Traill's original homestead.